Yoga Journal

This Book Belongs To

· ·

If Found, Please Call:

· ·

OM...

The Sound of the
Universe is my Original
Vibration

My Class Plan...

Level: ....

Duration: ....

Focus/Theme

_____

_____

Pose/Sequence

_____

_____

Props Required

_____

_____

Mantra/Playlist

_____

_____

Blessing of the Day

_____

_____

Date

....

My Class Plan...

Level: ....

Duration: ....

Focus/Theme

_____

_____

Pose/Sequence

_____

_____

Props Required

_____

_____

Mantra/Playlist

_____

_____

Blessing of the Day

_____

_____

Date

....

My Class Plan...

Level: ....

Duration: ....

Focus/Theme

Pose/Sequence

Props Required

Mantra/Playlist

Blessing of the Day

Date

....

My Class Plan...

Level: ....

Duration: ....

Focus/Theme

_____

_____

Pose/Sequence

_____

_____

Props Required

_____

_____

Mantra/Playlist

_____

_____

Blessing of the Day

_____

_____

Date

....

My Class Plan...

Level: ....

Duration: ....

Focus/Theme

_____

_____

Pose/Sequence

_____

_____

Props Required

_____

_____

Mantra/Playlist

_____

_____

Blessing of the Day

_____

_____

Date

....

My Class Plan...

Level: ....

Duration: ....

Focus/Theme

_____

_____

Pose/Sequence

_____

_____

Props Required

_____

_____

Mantra/Playlist

_____

_____

Blessing of the Day

_____

_____

Date

....

My Class Plan...

Level: ....

Duration: ....

Focus/Theme

Pose/Sequence

Props Required

Mantra/Playlist

Blessing of the Day

Date

....

My Class Plan...

Level: ....

Duration: ....

Focus/Theme

Pose/Sequence

Props Required

Mantra/Playlist

Blessing of the Day

Date

....

My Class Plan...

Level: ....

Duration: ....

Focus/Theme

_____

_____

Pose/Sequence

_____

_____

Props Required

_____

_____

Mantra/Playlist

_____

_____

Blessing of the Day

_____

_____

Date

....

My Class Plan...

Level: ....

Duration: ....

Focus/Theme

_____

_____

Pose/Sequence

_____

_____

Props Required

_____

_____

Mantra/Playlist

_____

_____

Blessing of the Day

_____

_____

Date

....

My Class Plan...

Level: ....

Duration: ....

Focus/Theme

_____

_____

Pose/Sequence

_____

_____

Props Required

_____

_____

Mantra/Playlist

_____

_____

Blessing of the Day

_____

_____

Date

....

My Class Plan...

Level: ....

Duration: ....

Focus/Theme

Pose/Sequence

Props Required

Mantra/Playlist

Blessing of the Day

Date

....

My Class Plan...

Level: ....

Duration: ....

Focus/Theme

_____

_____

Pose/Sequence

_____

_____

Props Required

_____

_____

Mantra/Playlist

_____

_____

Blessing of the Day

_____

_____

Date

....

My Class Plan...

Level: ....

Duration: ....

Focus/Theme

Pose/Sequence

Props Required

Mantra/Playlist

Blessing of the Day

Date

....

My Class Plan...

Level: ....

Duration: ....

Focus/Theme

Pose/Sequence

Props Required

Mantra/Playlist

Blessing of the Day

Date

....

My Class Plan...

Level: ....

Duration: ....

Focus/Theme

_____

_____

Pose/Sequence

_____

_____

Props Required

_____

_____

Mantra/Playlist

_____

_____

Blessing of the Day

_____

_____

Date

....

My Class Plan...

Level: ....

Duration: ....

Focus/Theme

_____

_____

Pose/Sequence

_____

_____

Props Required

_____

_____

Mantra/Playlist

_____

_____

Blessing of the Day

_____

_____

Date

....

My Class Plan...

Level: ....

Duration: ....

Focus/Theme

_____

_____

Pose/Sequence

_____

_____

Props Required

_____

_____

Mantra/Playlist

_____

_____

Blessing of the Day

_____

_____

Date

....

My Class Plan...

Level: ....

Duration: ....

Focus/Theme

_____

_____

Pose/Sequence

_____

_____

Props Required

_____

_____

Mantra/Playlist

_____

_____

Blessing of the Day

_____

_____

Date

....

My Class Plan...

Level: ....

Duration: ....

Focus/Theme

Pose/Sequence

Props Required

Mantra/Playlist

Blessing of the Day

Date

....

My Class Plan...

Level: ....

Duration: ....

Focus/Theme

Pose/Sequence

Props Required

Mantra/Playlist

Blessing of the Day

Date

....

My Class Plan...

Level: ....

Duration: ....

Focus/Theme

Pose/Sequence

Props Required

Mantra/Playlist

Blessing of the Day

Date

....

My Class Plan...

Level: ....

Duration: ....

Focus/Theme

Pose/Sequence

Props Required

Mantra/Playlist

Blessing of the Day

Date

....

My Class Plan...

Level: ....

Duration: ....

Focus/Theme

_____

_____

Pose/Sequence

_____

_____

Props Required

_____

Mantra/Playlist

_____

_____

Blessing of the Day

_____

_____

Date

....

My Class Plan...

Level: ....

Duration: ....

Focus/Theme

Pose/Sequence

Props Required

Mantra/Playlist

Blessing of the Day

Date

....

My Class Plan...

Level: ....

Duration: ....

Focus/Theme

_____

_____

Pose/Sequence

_____

_____

Props Required

_____

Mantra/Playlist

_____

_____

Blessing of the Day

_____

_____

Date

....

My Class Plan...

Level: ....

Duration: ....

Focus/Theme

_____

_____

Pose/Sequence

_____

_____

Props Required

_____

_____

Mantra/Playlist

_____

_____

Blessing of the Day

_____

_____

Date

....

My Class Plan...

Level: ....

Duration: ....

Focus/Theme

_____

_____

Pose/Sequence

_____

_____

Props Required

_____

_____

Mantra/Playlist

_____

_____

Blessing of the Day

_____

_____

Date

....

My Class Plan...

Level: ....

Duration: ....

Focus/Theme

Pose/Sequence

Props Required

Mantra/Playlist

Blessing of the Day

Date

....

My Class Plan...

Level: ....

Duration: ....

Focus/Theme

_____

_____

Pose/Sequence

_____

_____

Props Required

_____

_____

Mantra/Playlist

_____

_____

Blessing of the Day

_____

_____

Date

....

My Class Plan...

Level: ....

Duration: ....

Focus/Theme

Pose/Sequence

Props Required

Mantra/Playlist

Blessing of the Day

Date

....

My Class Plan...

Level: ....

Duration: ....

Focus/Theme

_____

_____

Pose/Sequence

_____

_____

Props Required

_____

_____

Mantra/Playlist

_____

_____

Blessing of the Day

_____

_____

Date

....

My Class Plan...

Level: ....

Duration: ....

Focus/Theme

_____

_____

Pose/Sequence

_____

_____

Props Required

_____

_____

Mantra/Playlist

_____

_____

Blessing of the Day

_____

_____

Date

....

My Class Plan...

Level: ....

Duration: ....

Focus/Theme

_____

_____

Pose/Sequence

_____

_____

Props Required

_____

_____

Mantra/Playlist

_____

_____

Blessing of the Day

_____

_____

Date

....

My Class Plan...

Level: ....

Duration: ....

Focus/Theme

Pose/Sequence

Props Required

Mantra/Playlist

Blessing of the Day

Date

....

My Class Plan...

Level: ....

Duration: ....

Focus/Theme

_____

_____

Pose/Sequence

_____

_____

Props Required

_____

_____

Mantra/Playlist

_____

_____

Blessing of the Day

_____

_____

Date

....

My Class Plan...

Level: ....

Duration: ....

Focus/Theme

Pose/Sequence

Props Required

Mantra/Playlist

Blessing of the Day

Date

....

My Class Plan...

Level: ....

Duration: ....

Focus/Theme

_____

_____

Pose/Sequence

_____

_____

Props Required

_____

_____

Mantra/Playlist

_____

_____

Blessing of the Day

_____

_____

Date

....

My Class Plan...

Level: ....

Duration: ....

Focus/Theme

Pose/Sequence

Props Required

Mantra/Playlist

Blessing of the Day

Date

....

My Class Plan...

Level: ....

Duration: ....

Focus/Theme

Pose/Sequence

Props Required

Mantra/Playlist

Blessing of the Day

Date

....

My Class Plan...

Level: ....

Duration: ....

Focus/Theme

_____

_____

Pose/Sequence

_____

_____

Props Required

_____

_____

Mantra/Playlist

_____

_____

Blessing of the Day

_____

_____

Date

....

My Class Plan...

Level: ....

Duration: ....

Focus/Theme

Pose/Sequence

Props Required

Mantra/Playlist

Blessing of the Day

Date

....

My Class Plan...

Level: ....

Duration: ....

Focus/Theme

_____

_____

Pose/Sequence

_____

_____

Props Required

_____

_____

Mantra/Playlist

_____

_____

Blessing of the Day

_____

_____

Date

....

My Class Plan...

Level: ....

Duration: ....

Focus/Theme

Pose/Sequence

Props Required

Mantra/Playlist

Blessing of the Day

Date

....

My Class Plan...

Level: ....

Duration: ....

Focus/Theme

Pose/Sequence

Props Required

Mantra/Playlist

Blessing of the Day

Date

....

My Class Plan...

Level: ....

Duration: ....

Focus/Theme

Pose/Sequence

Props Required

Mantra/Playlist

Blessing of the Day

Date

....

My Class Plan...

Level: ....

Duration: ....

Focus/Theme

_____

_____

Pose/Sequence

_____

_____

Props Required

_____

_____

Mantra/Playlist

_____

_____

Blessing of the Day

_____

Date

....

My Class Plan...

Level: ....

Duration: ....

Focus/Theme

Pose/Sequence

Props Required

Mantra/Playlist

Blessing of the Day

Date

....

My Class Plan...

Level: ....

Duration: ....

Focus/Theme

_____

_____

Pose/Sequence

_____

_____

Props Required

_____

_____

Mantra/Playlist

_____

_____

Blessing of the Day

_____

_____

Date

....

My Class Plan...

Level: ....

Duration: ....

Focus/Theme

Pose/Sequence

Props Required

Mantra/Playlist

Blessing of the Day

Date

....

My Class Plan...

Level: ....

Duration: ....

Focus/Theme

_____

_____

Pose/Sequence

_____

_____

Props Required

_____

_____

Mantra/Playlist

_____

_____

Blessing of the Day

_____

_____

Date

....

My Class Plan...

Level: ....

Duration: ....

Focus/Theme

Pose/Sequence

Props Required

Mantra/Playlist

Blessing of the Day

Date

....

My Class Plan...

Level: ....

Duration: ....

Focus/Theme

_____

_____

Pose/Sequence

_____

_____

Props Required

_____

_____

Mantra/Playlist

_____

_____

Blessing of the Day

_____

_____

Date

....

My Class Plan...

Level: ....

Duration: ....

Focus/Theme

Pose/Sequence

Props Required

Mantra/Playlist

Blessing of the Day

Date

....

My Class Plan...

Level: ....

Duration: ....

Focus/Theme

Pose/Sequence

Props Required

Mantra/Playlist

Blessing of the Day

Date

....

My Class Plan...

Level: ....

Duration: ....

Focus/Theme

Pose/Sequence

Props Required

Mantra/Playlist

Blessing of the Day

Date

....

My Class Plan...

Level: ....

Duration: ....

Focus/Theme

_____

_____

Pose/Sequence

_____

_____

Props Required

_____

_____

Mantra/Playlist

_____

_____

Blessing of the Day

_____

_____

Date

....

My Class Plan...

Level: ....

Duration: ....

Focus/Theme

Pose/Sequence

Props Required

Mantra/Playlist

Blessing of the Day

Date

....

My Class Plan...

Level: ....

Duration: ....

Focus/Theme

_____

_____

Pose/Sequence

_____

_____

Props Required

_____

_____

Mantra/Playlist

_____

_____

Blessing of the Day

_____

_____

Date

....

My Class Plan...

Level: ....

Duration: ....

Focus/Theme

Pose/Sequence

Props Required

Mantra/Playlist

Blessing of the Day

Date

....

My Class Plan...

Level: ....

Duration: ....

Focus/Theme

_____

_____

Pose/Sequence

_____

_____

Props Required

_____

_____

Mantra/Playlist

_____

_____

Blessing of the Day

_____

_____

Date

....

My Class Plan...

Level: ....

Duration: ....

Focus/Theme

Pose/Sequence

Props Required

Mantra/Playlist

Blessing of the Day

Date

....

My Class Plan...

Level: ....

Duration: ....

Focus/Theme

_____

_____

Pose/Sequence

_____

_____

Props Required

_____

_____

Mantra/Playlist

_____

_____

Blessing of the Day

_____

_____

Date

....

My Class Plan...

Level: ....

Duration: ....

Focus/Theme

Pose/Sequence

Props Required

Mantra/Playlist

Blessing of the Day

Date

....

My Class Plan...

Level: ....

Duration: ....

Focus/Theme

_____

_____

Pose/Sequence

_____

_____

Props Required

_____

_____

Mantra/Playlist

_____

_____

Blessing of the Day

_____

_____

Date

....

My Class Plan...

Level: ....

Duration: ....

Focus/Theme

_____

_____

Pose/Sequence

_____

_____

Props Required

_____

Mantra/Playlist

_____

_____

Blessing of the Day

_____

_____

Date

....

My Class Plan...

Level: ....

Duration: ....

Focus/Theme

Pose/Sequence

Props Required

Mantra/Playlist

Blessing of the Day

Date

....

My Class Plan...

Level: ....

Duration: ....

Focus/Theme

Pose/Sequence

Props Required

Mantra/Playlist

Blessing of the Day

Date

....

My Class Plan...

Level: ....

Duration: ....

Focus/Theme

Pose/Sequence

Props Required

Mantra/Playlist

Blessing of the Day

Date

....

My Class Plan...

Level: ....

Duration: ....

Focus/Theme

Pose/Sequence

Props Required

Mantra/Playlist

Blessing of the Day

Date

....

My Class Plan...

Level: ....

Duration: ....

Focus/Theme

Pose/Sequence

Props Required

Mantra/Playlist

Blessing of the Day

Date

....

My Class Plan...

Level: ....

Duration: ....

Focus/Theme

Pose/Sequence

Props Required

Mantra/Playlist

Blessing of the Day

Date

....

My Class Plan...

Level: ....

Duration: ....

Focus/Theme

Pose/Sequence

Props Required

Mantra/Playlist

Blessing of the Day

Date

....

My Class Plan...

Level: ....

Duration: ....

Focus/Theme

Pose/Sequence

Props Required

Mantra/Playlist

Blessing of the Day

Date

....

My Class Plan...

Level: ....

Duration: ....

Focus/Theme

Pose/Sequence

Props Required

Mantra/Playlist

Blessing of the Day

Date

....

My Class Plan...

Level: ....

Duration: ....

Focus/Theme

Pose/Sequence

Props Required

Mantra/Playlist

Blessing of the Day

Date

....

My Class Plan...

Level: ....

Duration: ....

Focus/Theme

_____

_____

Pose/Sequence

_____

_____

Props Required

_____

_____

Mantra/Playlist

_____

_____

Blessing of the Day

_____

_____

Date

....

My Class Plan...

Level: ....

Duration: ....

Focus/Theme

Pose/Sequence

Props Required

Mantra/Playlist

Blessing of the Day

Date

....

My Class Plan...

Level: ....

Duration: ....

Focus/Theme

Pose/Sequence

Props Required

Mantra/Playlist

Blessing of the Day

Date

....

My Class Plan...

Level: ....

Duration: ....

Focus/Theme

Pose/Sequence

Props Required

Mantra/Playlist

Blessing of the Day

Date

....

My Class Plan...

Level: ....

Duration: ....

Focus/Theme

_____

_____

Pose/Sequence

_____

_____

Props Required

_____

_____

Mantra/Playlist

_____

_____

Blessing of the Day

_____

_____

Date

....

My Class Plan...

Level: ....

Duration: ....

Focus/Theme

Pose/Sequence

Props Required

Mantra/Playlist

Blessing of the Day

Date

....

My Class Plan...

Level: ....

Duration: ....

Focus/Theme

Pose/Sequence

Props Required

Mantra/Playlist

Blessing of the Day

Date

....

My Class Plan...

Level: ....

Duration: ....

Focus/Theme

Pose/Sequence

Props Required

Mantra/Playlist

Blessing of the Day

Date

....

My Class Plan...

Level: ....

Duration: ....

Focus/Theme

Pose/Sequence

Props Required

Mantra/Playlist

Blessing of the Day

Date

....

My Class Plan...

Level: ....

Duration: ....

Focus/Theme

Pose/Sequence

Props Required

Mantra/Playlist

Blessing of the Day

Date

....

My Class Plan...

Level: ....

Duration: ....

Focus/Theme

Pose/Sequence

Props Required

Mantra/Playlist

Blessing of the Day

Date

....

My Class Plan...

Level: ....

Duration: ....

Focus/Theme

_____

_____

Pose/Sequence

_____

_____

Props Required

_____

_____

Mantra/Playlist

_____

_____

Blessing of the Day

_____

_____

Date

....

My Class Plan...

Level: ....

Duration: ....

Focus/Theme

Pose/Sequence

Props Required

Mantra/Playlist

Blessing of the Day

Date

....

My Class Plan...

Level: ....

Duration: ....

Focus/Theme

Pose/Sequence

Props Required

Mantra/Playlist

Blessing of the Day

Date

....

My Class Plan...

Level: ....

Duration: ....

Focus/Theme

_____

_____

Pose/Sequence

_____

_____

Props Required

_____

_____

Mantra/Playlist

_____

_____

Blessing of the Day

_____

_____

Date

....

My Class Plan...

Level: ....

Duration: ....

Focus/Theme

_____

_____

Pose/Sequence

_____

_____

Props Required

_____

Mantra/Playlist

_____

_____

Blessing of the Day

_____

_____

Date

....

My Class Plan...

Level: ....

Duration: ....

Focus/Theme

Pose/Sequence

Props Required

Mantra/Playlist

Blessing of the Day

Date

....

My Class Plan...

Level: ....

Duration: ....

Focus/Theme

Pose/Sequence

Props Required

Mantra/Playlist

Blessing of the Day

Date

....

My Class Plan...

Level: ....

Duration: ....

Focus/Theme

Pose/Sequence

Props Required

Mantra/Playlist

Blessing of the Day

Date

....

My Class Plan...

Level: ....

Duration: ....

Focus/Theme

_____

_____

Pose/Sequence

_____

_____

Props Required

_____

_____

Mantra/Playlist

_____

_____

Blessing of the Day

_____

_____

Date

....

My Class Plan...

Level: ....

Duration: ....

Focus/Theme

Pose/Sequence

Props Required

Mantra/Playlist

Blessing of the Day

Date

....

My Class Plan...

Level: ....

Duration: ....

Focus/Theme

Pose/Sequence

Props Required

Mantra/Playlist

Blessing of the Day

Date

....

My Class Plan...

Level: ....

Duration: ....

Focus/Theme

Pose/Sequence

Props Required

Mantra/Playlist

Blessing of the Day

Date

....

My Class Plan...

Level: ....

Duration: ....

Focus/Theme

Pose/Sequence

Props Required

Mantra/Playlist

Blessing of the Day

Date

....

My Class Plan...

Level: ....

Duration: ....

Focus/Theme

_____

_____

Pose/Sequence

_____

_____

Props Required

_____

_____

Mantra/Playlist

_____

_____

Blessing of the Day

_____

_____

Date

....

My Class Plan..

Level: ....

Duration: ....

Focus/Theme

Pose/Sequence

Props Required

Mantra/Playlist

Blessing of the Day

Date

....

My Class Plan...

Level: ....

Duration: ....

Focus/Theme

_____

_____

Pose/Sequence

_____

_____

Props Required

_____

_____

Mantra/Playlist

_____

_____

Blessing of the Day

_____

_____

Date

....

My Class Plan..

Level: ....

Duration: ....

Focus/Theme

Pose/Sequence

Props Required

Mantra/Playlist

Blessing of the Day

Date

....

My Class Plan...

Level: ....

Duration: ....

Focus/Theme

Pose/Sequence

Props Required

Mantra/Playlist

Blessing of the Day

Date

....

My Class Plan..

Level: ....

Duration: ....

Focus/Theme

_____

_____

Pose/Sequence

_____

Props Required

_____

Mantra/Playlist

_____

Blessing of the Day

_____

_____

Date

....

My Class Plan...

Level: ....

Duration: ....

Focus/Theme

Pose/Sequence

Props Required

Mantra/Playlist

Blessing of the Day

Date

....

My Class Plan..

Level: ....

Duration: ....

Focus/Theme

Pose/Sequence

Props Required

Mantra/Playlist

Blessing of the Day

Date

....

My Class Plan...

Level: ....

Duration: ....

Focus/Theme

Pose/Sequence

Props Required

Mantra/Playlist

Blessing of the Day

Date

....

My Class Plan...

Level: ....

Duration: ....

Focus/Theme

Pose/Sequence

Props Required

Mantra/Playlist

Blessing of the Day

Date

....

My Class Plan...

Level: ....

Duration: ....

Focus/Theme

Pose/Sequence

Props Required

Mantra/Playlist

Blessing of the Day

Date

....

My Class Plan..

Level: ....

Duration: ....

Focus/Theme

Pose/Sequence

Props Required

Mantra/Playlist

Blessing of the Day

Date

....

My Class Plan...

Level: ....

Duration: ....

Focus/Theme

Pose/Sequence

Props Required

Mantra/Playlist

Blessing of the Day

Date

....

My Class Plan...

Level: ....

Duration: ....

Focus/Theme

_____

_____

Pose/Sequence

_____

_____

Props Required

_____

_____

Mantra/Playlist

_____

_____

Blessing of the Day

_____

_____

Date

....

My Class Plan...

Level: ....

Duration: ....

Focus/Theme

_____

_____

Pose/Sequence

_____

_____

Props Required

_____

_____

Mantra/Playlist

_____

_____

Blessing of the Day

_____

_____

Date

....

My Class Plan

Level: ....

Duration: ....

Focus/Theme

Pose/Sequence

Props Required

Mantra/Playlist

Blessing of the Day

Date

....

My Class Plan...

Level: ....

Duration: ....

Focus/Theme

Pose/Sequence

Props Required

Mantra/Playlist

Blessing of the Day

Date

....

My Class Plan..

Level: ....

Duration: ....

Focus/Theme

Pose/Sequence

Props Required

Mantra/Playlist

Blessing of the Day

Date

....

My Class Plan...

Level: ....

Duration: ....

Focus/Theme

Pose/Sequence

Props Required

Mantra/Playlist

Blessing of the Day

Date

....

My Class Plan...

Level: ....

Duration: ....

Focus/Theme

_____

_____

Pose/Sequence

_____

Props Required

_____

Mantra/Playlist

_____

_____

Blessing of the Day

_____

_____

Date

....